Luna and the Spark of Wonder
First Edition, May 2025
Text Copyright © 2025 Joe Sarkic
Illustration Copyright © 2025 Joe Sarkic
Seeds of Wonder Series Logo © 2025 Joe Sarkic
Published by Joe Sarkic

All rights reserved.

ISBN: 978-1-7382525-9-6

The images and the content of this book are protected by copyright. No part of this book may be reproduced, distributed, or transmitted in any form or by any means, including photocopying, recording, or other electronic or mechanical methods, without the prior written permission of the copyright owner.

This book is intended for entertainment and educational purposes only. The characters and events portrayed in this book are fictitious. Any similarity to real persons, living or dead, is purely coincidental.

Dedication

For all the little wonder-seekers who turn their heads skyward and whisper "Why?"—may your questions light the path to new adventures, and may each answer you discover fuel the spark of your imagination

Luna and the Spark of Wonder

Joe Sarkic

A Message for the Parents

Luna and the Spark of Wonder is a children's book for ages 3 to 5 that combines poetic language with a rich visual narrative. At its heart, it tells the story of Luna, a curious child who captures her "Why?" questions in a glowing jar that lights up her nights with mystery. Each evening, under a silver moon, she tucks a freshly penned note into the jar and follows the gentle guidance of Professor Owlbright on flights through starlit skies and shadowed gardens. As she learns why stars shimmer, why clouds blush at sunset, and why shooting sparks streak the heavens, the jar pulses with new light—showing young readers that curiosity can spark discovery and that patience, exploration, and gentle guidance can transform a simple question into a grand adventure of learning.

More information about how you can support your child during reading time can be found in the back of the book.

Parental Learning Support

Broaden your child's engagement with Luna and the Spark of Wonder by bringing the story's curiosity and discovery into your home:

1. Ask Reflective Questions:

- "Why do you think Luna chooses a new question each night for her jar?"
- "If you could capture any 'Why?' in a glowing jar, what would you ask?"

2. Encourage Asking Questions:

Nightly Question Activity: Offer an empty jar, strips of paper, and glow-in-the-dark markers or colored pencils. Invite your child to write one question, with your help, and tuck it inside before bed. Replace the question slip with an answer after your child has fallen asleep.

3. Use the Moral Lessons as Prompts for Conversation:

Throughout Luna's journey, themes of curiosity, patience, exploration, and gentle guidance emerge. At key points, pause and ask:

- "What new things have you discovered by asking questions?"
- "How can we help each other learn, like Professor Owlbright helps Luna?"

Luna put her cheek against the jar of questions, watching moonbeams shimmer across the tiny notes inside.

Each note began with "Why?" and each question shone like a little star.

She wondered if she would ever know all the answers.

Asking questions helps you learn new things.

Before bedtime, she wrote another "Why do clouds float in the sky?"

Her little fingers shook as she tucked it into the jar's pile of notes.

The jar's lid rattled softly, waiting for more questions.

Small questions can spark big wonder.

At night, the jar glowed brighter, and Luna heard a "HOOT" outside.

She wanted to find out why?, so she stepped into the garden.

A gentle breeze carried the smell of night flowers as she tiptoed toward an old oak tree.

Nighttime has secrets to explore.

Up in the oak tree, Professor Owlbright blinked his bright eyes at Luna.

He wore round glasses that shone in the moonlight.

"You can ask me any question," he hooted softly.

Kind teachers help us learn.

Luna chose her question. "**Why do stars twinkle?**" she asked.

Owlbright pointed his wing to the sky.

"**The stars twinkle,**" he said softly, "**because the wind up high makes their light wiggle.**"

Asking questions helps us learn new things.

Big Dipper

Orion

He helped her count the big, bright stars and told her their names.

Luna wrote each name on a new note and tucked it into the jar.

With each new name, the jar beats like a little heart.

Writing things down helps us remember better.

When night got dark, Owlbright hooted a soft lullaby.

Luna closed her eyes and let the song make pictures in her head.

When she opened her eyes, she saw the jar glowing twice as bright.

Our imagination shines when we stop and listen.

Then Luna asked, "Why do clouds turn golden at sunset?"

He pointed to the sky where clouds had pink and gold edges.

He said the sun's light paints the sky with color.

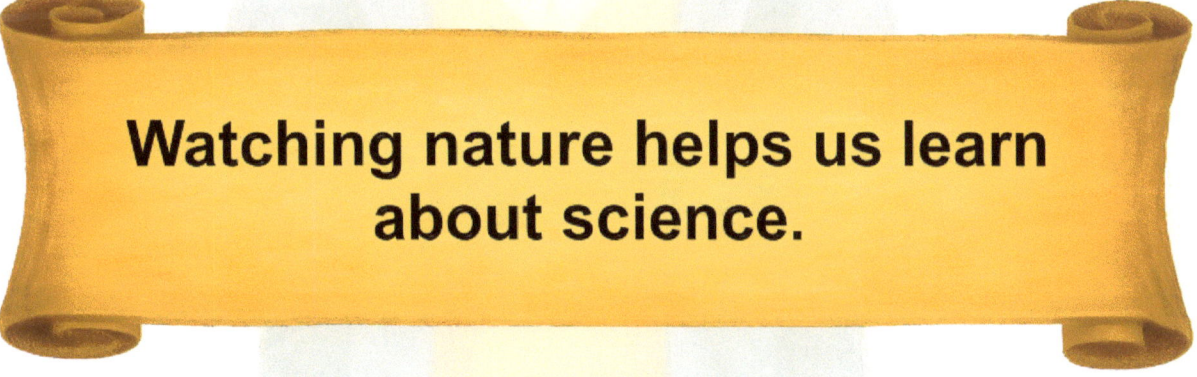

Watching nature helps us learn about science.

The jar shook, waiting for more questions, and Luna smiled and felt sleepy.

Owlbright spread his big wings to shelter her from the breeze.

In the quiet, she wrote down the answer about clouds.

Feeling safe helps our minds rest and learn.

When morning came, Luna closed the jar lid and thanked her teacher.

The first birds began to sing in the morning air.

She fell asleep on soft grass.

Sleeping helps our minds feel fresh.

When the sun rose, Luna saw the jar glowing with soft green light.

She opened it and saw new notes glowing with soft color.

Each answer felt like a new adventure.

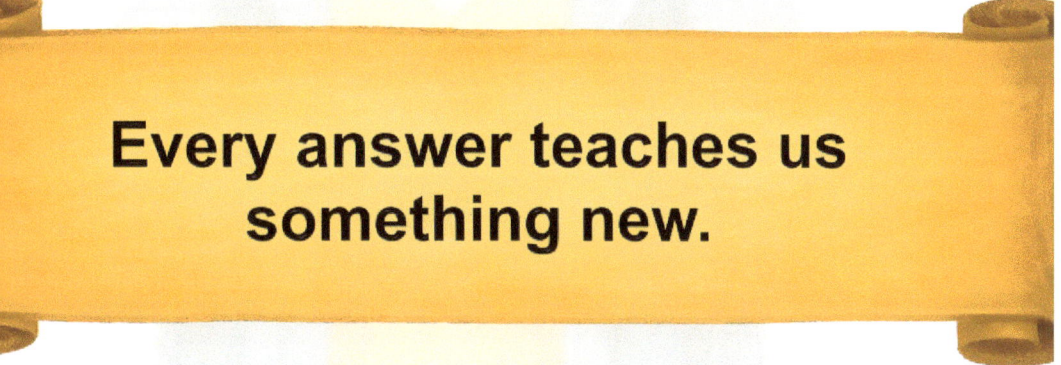

Every answer teaches us something new.

One night, Luna asked Owlbright, "Why did I see a bright streak in the sky?"

He pointed at a spark zooming through the night.

"A shooting star is a little rock from space that burns up and glows like a spark as it flies through the sky," he said.

Shooting stars help us remember that beautiful things don't last long.

She counted shooting stars and saw each one glowed just once.

Her jar looked happy with each new surprise.

Luna felt like the sky was sharing its secrets.

Nature shares its secrets when we look.

Owlbright pointed at the moon's round spots.

Luna drew the moon with its round spots until she felt sleepy.

The jar felt warm in her lap.

Looking closely helps us pay attention.

As a final night lesson, Luna asked, "Why do fireflies glow in the dark?"

The professor whispered. "Fireflies glow to find friends and light up the night."

Luna tucked the glowing answer into her jar, which pulsed softly.

Even small lights can show the way.

When the owl stopped hooting, Luna closed her eyes under the stars.

The jar glowed bright, like it was full of moonlight.

She dreamed about sharing all her answers.

Dreams help us remember what we learn.

Morning light filled her room, and Luna woke up happy.

She opened the jar and saw each note glowing green.

A soft breeze brought new questions.

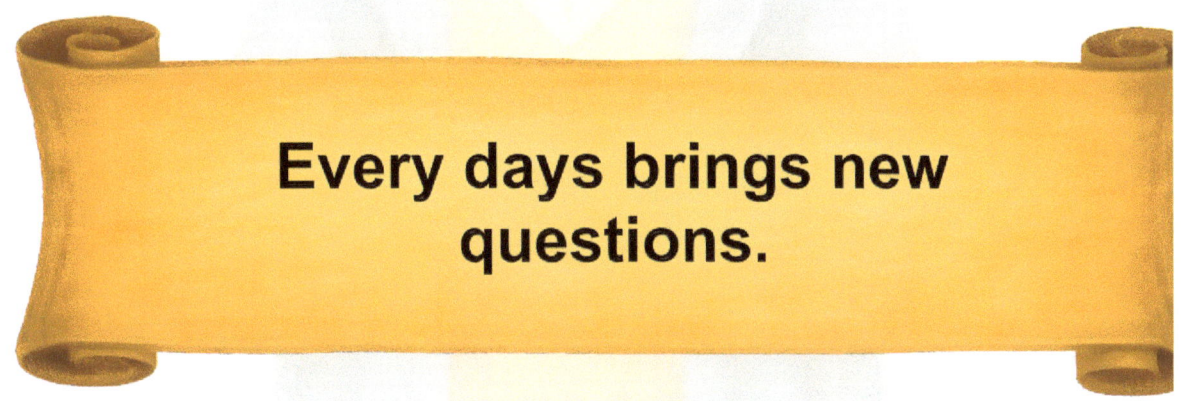

Every days brings new questions.

At school, Luna showed her glowing jar to her friends.

They leaned close with big eyes.

She told them about clouds and stars, and they all said, "Wow!"

Then everyone started asking their own "Why?" questions.

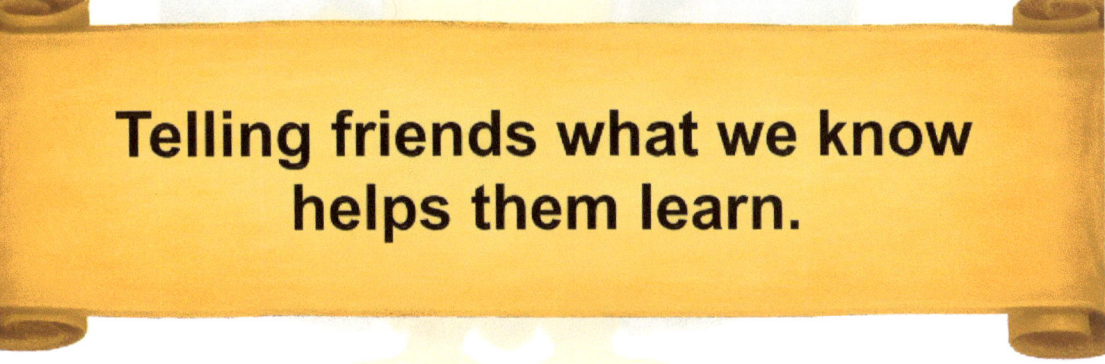

Telling friends what we know helps them learn.

By day's end, the town was alive with curious voices, each child chasing answers in books and gardens.

Luna watched from her window, her jar softly humming in her lap.

She realized that asking questions was the greatest adventure of all.

Collective curiosity transforms communities.

Luna forgot to ask Professor Owlbright, "Why do clouds float in the sky?"

To help you find an answer, find a grown-up to help you do an experiment:

1. Make your bubble mix:

Pour a little water into a small bowl and stir in a few drops of dish soap.

2. Blow your clouds:

Dip a straw or bubble wand into the mix and blow gently to create lots of little bubbles.

3. Watch them float:

Let the bubbles drift—see how they hover in the air just like clouds.

4. Ask and share:

Talk about *why* the bubbles float. Then explain that clouds are made of tiny drops of water that float in the sky just like your bubbles.

Finally, tell a grown-up or friend what you discovered!

> **It's okay to ask grown-ups or books for answers.**
>
> **Telling others what we learn helps them too.**

What the Book Teaches

1. **Curiosity and Discovery**

   - Luna's nightly "Why?" questions send her and Professor Owlbright soaring into moonlit skies and secret gardens.
   - **Lesson for kids**: Asking "Why?" lights up your world with new adventures.
   - **Lesson for parents**: Celebrate and encourage your child's questions—each one can spark a journey of discovery.

2. **Patience and Reflection**

   - As Luna tucks her question into the glowing jar, she waits for its soft pulse to reveal an answer.
   - Lesson for kids: Sometimes the best answers come when you're willing to wait and listen.
   - Lesson for parents: Model calm patience—show that reflecting on questions is as important as asking them.

3. **Exploration and Learning**

   - Under Owlbright's gentle guidance, Luna learns why stars shimmer and clouds blush, exploring mysteries beyond her window.

- **Lesson for kids**: Exploring new places and ideas helps you understand the world around you
- **Lesson for parents**: Take time to explore alongside your child—whether it's stargazing in the backyard or reading about nature's wonders.

4. **Mentorship and Guidance**

   - Professor Owlbright shares wisdom, helping Luna transform a simple question into a glowing revelation.
   - **Lesson for kids**: Learning from someone wise can turn confusion into clarity.
   - **Lesson for parents**: Offer gentle guidance and share your own curiosity—being a mentor builds confidence and wonder.

5. **Imagination and Creative Expression**

   - The jar's glowing light pulses in colors that mirror Luna's growing understanding and imagination.
   - **Lesson for kids:** Your imagination can color questions with wonder and make every answer feel magical.
   - **Lesson for parents:** Provide tools—jars, markers, paper—to help your child capture their own "**Why?**" ideas and bring them to light.

Final Summary for Parents

Luna and the Spark of Wonder offers a luminous, engaging tale that nurtures your child's curiosity and reflective thinking through nightly "Why?" adventures with Luna and her wise owl guide, introducing foundational literacy and scientific inquiry via poetic language and vivid imagery. Its emphasis on patience, gentle mentorship, and imaginative exploration creates natural opportunities to discuss empathy, perseverance, and the magic of questioning. Sharing this book enriches language development, critical thinking, and parent–child bonding as you celebrate each question, discovery, and the wonder that lights even the darkest night.

Author Bio

Joe Sarkic lives in Ottawa, Canada, with his wife and two teenage children—the everyday heroes who inspire many of his stories.

With degrees in Physics from the University of Waterloo and Computer Science from the University of Ottawa, Joe has built a distinguished career in software and systems engineering. Yet it's within the pages of fantasy and science fiction that he truly finds himself, weaving tales that transport readers to distant realms and spark the imagination.

Joe also nurtures a deep passion for children's storytelling, believing in the quiet power of stories to inspire wonder, kindness, and resilience in young minds.

To discover more about me — including other books I've authored and new projects taking shape — visit **www.sarkic.com** or scan the QR code below.

Thank you for walking these pages with me — if the story stayed with you, I invite you to leave a review on Amazon by scanning the QR code below for the U.S. or Canada, or by searching for the title in your country's Amazon app.

Amazon U.S.   **Amazon Canada**

Continue the adventure in the *Seeds of Wonder Series*.
More magical journeys await!

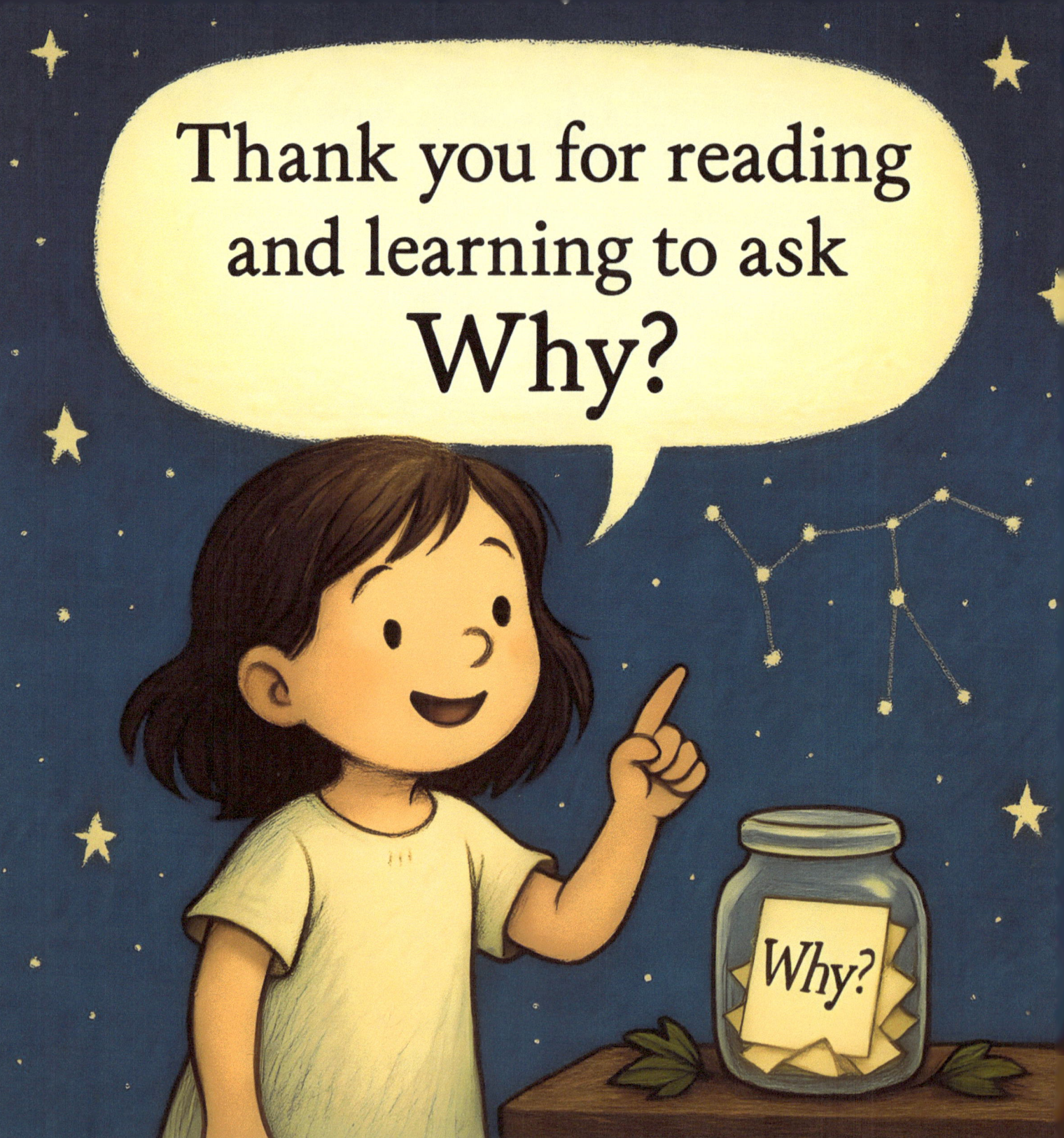